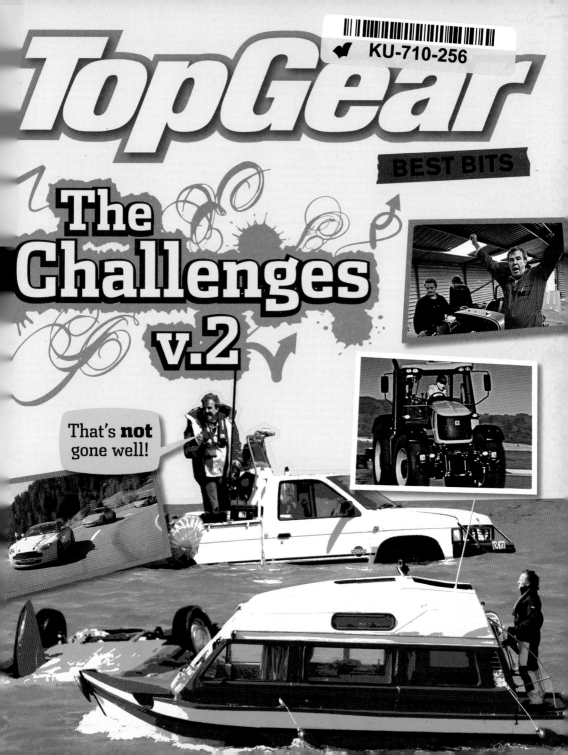

TopGear

BEST BITS

The Challenges v.2

That's **not** gone well!

BBC Children's Books
Published by the Penguin Group
Penguin Books Ltd, 80 Strand, London WC2R 0RL, England
Penguin Group (Australia) Ltd, 250 Camberwell Road,
Camberwell, Victoria 3124, Australia (a division of Pearson
Australia Group Pty Ltd)
Canada, India, New Zealand, South Africa

Published by BBC Children's Books, 2009
Text and design © Children's Character Books, 2009

10 9 8 7 6 5 4 3 2 1

791.457
Top

Written by Mark Hillsdon

ISBN: 978-1-40590-542-8

Printed in China

Quite scared. **Quite scared.
Quite really scared.**

Contents

There's nothing for it, I'm going to **deploy my Boadiceas!**

This is the **third time** I've been **in this ruddy sea.**

Introduction

The Top Gear Challenges have become the stuff of legend. In fact they've even been debated in the House of Commons, with one Honourable Member talking about the 'presenters' silly and foolish antics. How dare he!

This time around we've got six more stupendous challenges for you to enjoy.

First up, the lads try and help out the British Bobby with some suggestions about how to improve the standard police car. The results should have crims quaking in their boots!

Then it's off to Europe in a new breed of supercar to find the best stretch of road ever laid. If you're feeling a bit delicate, we suggest you avoid the pictures of James driving in the buff!

After that it's back to the water for the second Top Gear Amphibious Car Challenge, where once again Jeremy's power overcomes the 'sailing skills' of Richard and James.

Top Gear tries to go a bit green next, by taking on a challenge to grow its own petrol. However, it's not long before the good intentions start to play second fiddle to some monster tractors, a ploughman's lunch and some dynamite!

Our heroic trio take on the Stig in the Build A Car Challenge, with the speed meister charging up from Surrey as our mechanical masterminds try and build a Caterham Seven from scratch.

So how hard can it be? Let's find out!

The World's Best Driving Road

The Challenge

This was a mission to find the best driving road in the world, as well as to decide whether the new breed of super-light supercars were really worth all the fuss – and the extra dosh. It also turned out to be a story of Jeremy's gas guzzling monster, Richard's dodgy map reading and James' poor numb bum.

Where is the **best driving road in the world?** Something that has everything, the **challenging** bends, no traffic, great views, the **long fast straight,** the lot.

South of France

The team pored over a map of the world and finally decided that their quest for the Holy Grail of driving would centre on the Alps and start in the south of France.

The Cars

Richard plumped for the Porsche 911 GT3 RS, which he modestly described as the world's ultimate version of the ultimate supercar, even if it was lurid green.

Jeremy chose the slightly eccentric Lamborghini Gallardo Superleggera, in a fetching shade of day-glo orange, with a V10 engine under the bonnet.

James, however, went the whole hog. On the surface his bright yellow Aston Martin looked fine, but a quick peek through the window revealed he'd stripped it back to the bare minimum to make it even lighter.

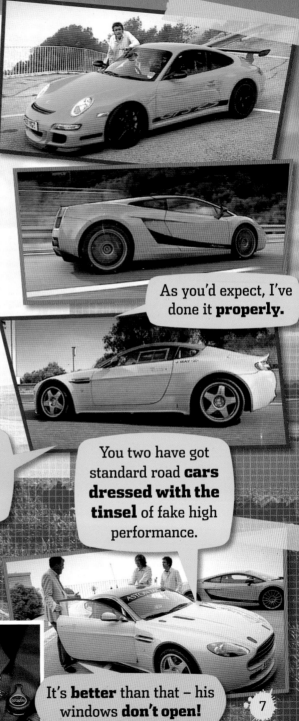

As you'd expect, I've done it **properly.**

James, you have got a car with **no air conditioning,** in the south of France, in the **middle of summer!**

You two have got standard road **cars dressed with the tinsel** of fake high performance.

It's **better** than that – his windows **don't open!**

And they're off!

Or at least Richard and Jeremy were. James was already lagging behind after trying to find out which combination of switches actually started the car, while at the same time trying to strap himself into his racing harness.

I've done **three minutes** and I already **adore this car!**

ZZOOOOOMMM!

Col De Turini

First stop was the Col De Turini, a stretch of road that's used as a special stage in the legendary Monte Carlo rally, in the South of France. It looked like the ideal place to unleash the cars.

So much fun!

A ribbon of tarmac that doesn't really go anywhere. So it was **quiet – till we arrived.**

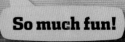

Col De Turini

Monaco

James' Aston

It was very admirable of James to take out all the little luxuries from his Aston in an attempt to get back in touch with what driving was all about. But it was making for a pretty rough ride! And he was soon beginning to regret getting rid of the air con, as he was starting to get hot, very hot.

They're **so smug** about their **fancy boy versions** of lightweight cars.

KSSsH!

You can **hear** all the **machinery working** and **you can feel** what it does.

CLUNK!

It's **busy.** It's **twisty,** it's got low walls that you can go over – **huge drops that can kill you with ease.**

James wasn't so convinced, and the harder he drove to catch up the more unbearable the noise inside his Aston became.

VRROOOMM

What a road!

Jeremy and Richard were so far ahead of James that they decided to pull over and discuss their cars. Meanwhile, back in the Aston James was hot and uncomfortable, with numb buttocks, a sweaty shirt and smelly pits. And he was sitting so low in his seat that he felt like an 85-year-old man!

I'm now beginning to go **slightly faint** as a result **dehydration**

My **eardrums** are **bleeding**...it's going to **kill me.**

2 LACETS

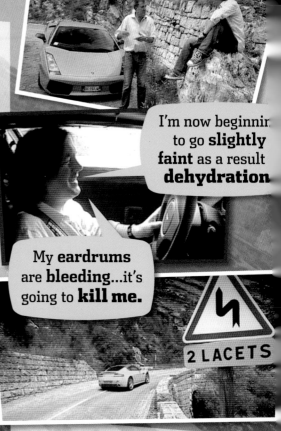

PZZZEOooMMMM!

The **trouble** with **tunnel blasting** in a car with **atomic power** like the Lambo is that the **fuel economy** does **drop** a bit. I was doing 9 miles to the gallon.

Once James finally joined the others, they all agreed that the Col De Turini had set a good benchmark but felt sure there were even better roads just around the corner. So, much to James' dismay, they set off for the Italian Riviera where the road wasn't much but there were some perks. Tunnels! The cars made an amazing amount of noise - it was a symphony to Jeremy's ears.

While they filled up, James bought himself a cushion to ease his aching bum, not that he would admit it.

Let me guess, that's **interior design,** it's a scatter cushion to look **pretty.**

This **doesn't look** like a **very good town.** They're going to **shout** at me.

How could this be worse?

It could be **worse.**

That night they stopped off at a rough looking hotel that Jeremy had booked.

We're **staying here** tonight?

Well, yes.

So we're carrying on by **bicycle tomorrow** are we, because these will have been **stolen, obviously.**

The Italian Lakes

The next day they arrived in the stunning Italian Lakes – and drove straight into a traffic jam. Richard and James were not best pleased.

Essentially he's brought u up somebody' drive way.

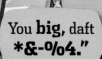

You **big,** daft ***&-%4."**

This road is rubbish.

I'm exploring the limits of grip here.

And it was a speed hump that broke the camel's back.

Eventually they eased their way through the traffic and caught the ferry across the lakes but on the other side James' Aston wouldn't start. In the end the others had to push him off – "at least it's light," quipped James, before realizing he hadn't turned the fuel pump on!

Jeremy was getting annoyed at all the beeping. "It's your country that makes supercars so you can't honk when somebody actually goes and buys one!"

> **The Swiss** will look on these three cars as if **the anti-christ has come** to their little world.

Switzerland

The road on the other side of the lake was a boring dual carriageway but it did lead to Switzerland and the magnificent San Bernardino Pass. The views were stunning and the lads were happy that they'd found an awesome stretch of road. The only problem was that the Swiss are sticklers for speed limits.

> The **hills are alive** with the **sound of horsepower.**

PAAARRRRRP

> **I fear** I may have made a **slight mistake** here.

Next, Richard convinced the others to keep heading north and they soon arrived in Liechtenstein, a tax haven where, apparently, they make more false teeth than anywhere else in the world.

But then disaster - the road ahead was closed for a cycling race.

Switzerland...again

They then headed back through Switzerland and the ski resort town of Davos. Jeremy and Richard decided to vandalize James' car to lighten the mood after a very long day.

Perfection

Then, south of Davos it happened. They found it. The perfect stretch of road. A true test of brakes, steering, grip, power and handling.

But not everyone was so happy.

> This is **absolute heaven.**

> What was God thinking of when he gave **the Swiss** this place – plainly it **should be ours.**

> This is **much more like it.**

> I wonder **how much more** of this I have to endure before I can admit that **this is a terrible car and that I hate it** and that I want to go home.

> Jeremy Clarkson today **married a Lamborghini** and moved to Switzerland.

> Everything about **this car now has come alive.** It's suddenly **in its element.**

> Shall we **do it?**

The Cherry on Top

They'd all pretty much decided that they'd found driving heaven, well, two of them did... but then, as they crossed over into Italy, a cherry on top of the cake! The Stelvio Pass came into view. It was fifteen miles of asphalt spaghetti draped on an alp and it was stunning.

> What an extraordinary road – **thank you Italy.**

> There's no other way of saying it, this is a **magnificent piece of road building.**

> o over the edge here and you'd **have time to phone the insurers!**

ZZOOOOOMMM!

And at last they all agreed on something!

> This is **hard work.** If I had no air con **I'd look ridiculous now.**

The Final Verdict

Davos to Stelvio – the greatest driving road in the world.

And as for the supercars, the team were a bit confused as to why you end up paying more for a car with less.

> We took **three cars** on holiday and they were **all wrong.**

Making a Better Police Car

The Challenge

The Top Gear team were a bit concerned for the humble British bobby. Unlike their American counterparts, who seem to love crashing their cars in tyre squealing chases, our coppers mustn't even scratch theirs.

The British police daren't crash their cars because they haven't got **enough money to fix** them up again.

So our three would-be law enforcers set out to put things right. Each were given £1000 to spend on a second-hand car that they thought could successfully replace the £9000 Astra Diesel the police currently use. And the beauty was that because they were just cheap, used cars, it didn't matter if they got a bit smashed up.

The Cars

Jeremy turned up in a sporty Fiat Coupe, that had a top speed of 152mph (so he claimed) and cost him just £900.

James on the other hand, went for safe, sensible and Masonic, arriving in a £900 Lexus.

Then, as they were arguing over which car was best, Richard appeared in a Suzuki Vitara jeep that he claimed was a budget (but nifty!) version of the Land Rover.

Officer Barbie has arrived!

ROZZERS

tching crims and locking them up...

...in your community

FZZZZHH!!

They were given a further £500 to turn their vehicles into the perfect modern police car and then told to rendez-vous at the legendary Top Gear track where they would be set a series of challenges.

James went for a classic British look, with stripes down each side and a simple blue flashing light. His secret weapon was a set of nozzles that could spray pink paint. And if that wasn't bad enough, his siren had been borrowed from an old ice cream van.

Feast on **my magnificence.**

Then Jeremy arrived.

Jeremy's car did look good, like something the Italian police would use in a high-speed chase. And his secret weapon was a vicious pair of metal spikes stuck to his back wheels.

Richard went for lots of blue flashing lights with a special 'stinger' attached to the front. On closer inspection it was actually just an old piece of carpet with some nails sticking through it. Once the Hamster 'activated' it, it would roll out in front of the crim's car and burst the tyres. Well, that was the theory!

IN JAIL NO ONE CAN HEAR YOU SCREAM

CLUNK! CLUN

It was **unmistakably** a **doormat with some nails** in it!

Police

Call 999 for details

The Speed Test

First the Stig did a lap in a standard police car, clocking a time of 1.48. Next up were the TG posse of lawmen, with extra points awarded for flamboyant driving.

James got off to a typically slow start, and then threw in a bit of tyre squeal for effect. The others scoffed at his time of 2.03 seconds.

I can hear a lot of noise but not a lot of movement – it's very **much like Jeremy really.**

I hope you **like prison food crims.**

CRASH

Jeremy covered the camera lens with Vaseline for a 'soft focus' effect before starting his lap with a dramatic J-turn in his car, but then stalled it. His spikes didn't exactly help the handling and he came over the line in 2.8 seconds.

So what could Richard do? He decided to give up on speed and went off road to try and earn some extra points. He crashed through a handily placed wall of cardboard boxes to put him ahead in the flamboyance stakes.

The others were impressed but by the time Richard crossed the line, his engine had given up and the watch had stopped at 3.14 seconds.

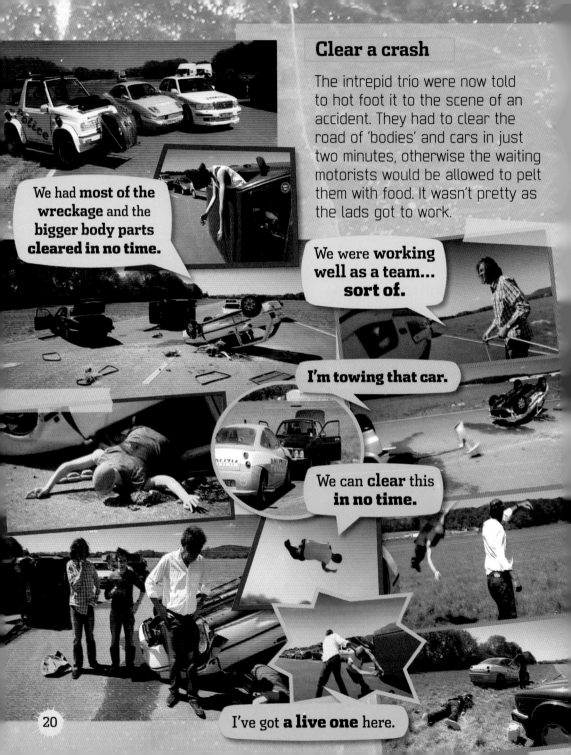

Clear a crash

The intrepid trio were now told to hot foot it to the scene of an accident. They had to clear the road of 'bodies' and cars in just two minutes, otherwise the waiting motorists would be allowed to pelt them with food. It wasn't pretty as the lads got to work.

We had **most of the wreckage** and the **bigger body parts cleared in no time.**

We were **working well as a team... sort of.**

I'm towing that car.

We can **clear** this **in no time.**

I've got **a live one** here.

Catching a crim

The final test involved the would-be rozzers showing the real PC Plods how their cheap cars could be used to stop a stolen vehicle. One of several problems facing them, however, was the fact that the stolen car was being driven by Ronnie Stigs.

Inspector Morose went first, eager to test out his paint guns.

How long have you got before you have to **go home tonight?**

That's **brilliant.**

I'm **amazed.**

He's pounced!

A-POWWW

Oh, I say, **it's worked.** Right on the windscreen.

In order to use his paint sprayers James had to get in front of the villain. Instead of chasing him, he 'cleverly' lay in wait then pulled out just before the Stig went past. The paint worked brilliantly and for nearly a whole second the Stig looked like he was going to be nicked. Then he turned on his windscreen wipers...

Come on, give chase.

I'm a **police officer,** I shall **never give up.**

Richard was up next.

That's **pathetic.**

Once again Richard went off road to intercept the Stig and deployed his stinger. But it was far too short and the Stig simply drove round it!

There's nothing for it, **I'm going to deploy my Boadiceas!**

Last but not least was Jeremy, who began his pursuit by trying to push the Stig off the road. When that failed he went for his secret weapon.

He then rammed them into the side of the Stig's BMW.

That's **uncomfortable.**

CRASH!

Yep.

ARRRGGH!

I presume, at some point, there's going to be a simply **hideous accident.**

Then Jeremy's wheel flew off, almost taking Richard's legs with it.

Something's **gone wrong with the handling!**

Result

So, to the final reckoning. The Top Gear score board showed James in third place, Jeremy in second and Richard in first, conveniently winning by one point. Before Jeremy was able to argue, the Hamster stuffed the evidence into his mouth!

	Cost	Speed	Flamboyance	Arrest The Stig	TOTAL
JAMES Lexus	100	-12	0	0	88
JEREMY Fiat	100	-20	0	98	178
RICHARD Suzuki	250	-72	1	0	179

We have to **conclude** that **the best car** for the **British police is a Suzuki Vitara** with a doormat on the front.

You've eaten it!

KKRNTCH

Yes **I have!**

23

Amphibious Car Challenge
Return to the water!

The Challenge

Having failed miserably to sail a car across a reservoir in Staffordshire, the top dogs at Top Gear decided to make the lads go back to the drawing board, refine their amphibious cars and have another go.

The Cars

Last time around, Jeremy's Toybota flipped over just before the finish line, so this time he added a couple of oil drums to his Nissan, or rather his Nissank, to try and make it more stable.

This **will sink** within **30 feet.**

As for Richard's Dampervan, it was now sporting a huge fibreglass hull – although unfortunately the Hamster couldn't see over the top to steer.

This **won't** work.

Both Richard and Jeremy had used bucket loads of squirty foam in the hopes of keeping their 'boats' more water tight.

Some time later, Captain Pugwash arrived in his Triumph Herald, which this time had a collapsible mast and various other devices that James claimed would help him steer.

Dover to Calais

The intrepid sailors discovered that this time their challenge was to take on the English Channel and sail the 22 miles from Dover to Calais on the French coast. It was a challenge that even knocked the wind out of Jeremy's sails!

We're **all** going to be **killed.**

If I'd known it was e sea I'd have fitted **bigger anchor.**

I can't believe they're asking us to **cross the** **Channel** in them.

On the drive to Dover, things started to go wrong. Richard's car began to fill with smoke as the hot engine began to melt all that foam. And surprise, surprise, so did Jeremy's.

Ruined!

How's your engine?

FZZZZHH!!

This is fantastic. I absolutely **cannot wait** to try out my Triumph Herald... **why shouldn't it work?**

For once it was James who was the most confident – although no-one was sure why. But he did feel the need to drive with a fire extinguisher in one hand...just in case.

25

Once in Dover, our three salty sea dogs stood staring out to sea. Inside the harbour all was calm, but outside the safety of those big stone walls, things we're very different. Oh, and did we mention that the English Channel is the busiest shipping lane in the world? It's full of massive tankers and huge ferries! Not surprisingly it didn't take long for the lads to decide that there wasn't time to attempt a crossing that night, so they all trooped off to the pub.

The next morning Captain May was keen to get going.

The others, however, weren't, and they began to come up with all kinds of ideas to stop them having to enter the water...

It's **all ship shape** and **ready to go.**

Have you **ever considered the meaning of life?**

No, but I think **we should.**

...including counting the individual granules in a teaspoon of sugar.

Yeah, **I lost count.** I want to **get it right.**

You've started **again.**

And **now's the time.**

Finally, two and three-quarter hours later, Richard and Jeremy joined James on the slipway. But the delaying tactics continued, with Jeremy checking that the hydrofoil bin lids he'd stuck to the car the previous night were still there.

Fed up with waiting, James went for it. And he was soon wishing he hadn't!

DOOFF

Unable to steer, James looked on course for a collision with the pier. Luckily a rescue boat arrived and nudged the Triumph back into open water.

Mayday!

I'm **enjoying** this!

You're being **rescued** after a minute and a half!

It's **so unfair.**

SPALOOSSHH

He's going down. I think **we should get in there.**

But after another minute and a half James started sinking but in true maritime tradition, his fellow sailors were soon on the scene trying to 'rescue' him.

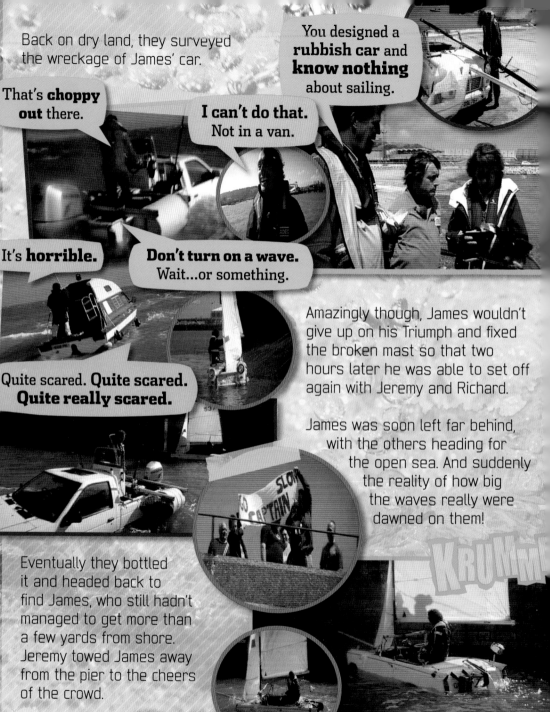

Back on dry land, they surveyed the wreckage of James' car.

You designed a **rubbish car** and **know nothing** about sailing.

That's **choppy out** there.

I can't do that. Not in a van.

It's **horrible.**

Don't turn on a wave. Wait...or something.

Quite scared. **Quite scared. Quite really scared.**

Amazingly though, James wouldn't give up on his Triumph and fixed the broken mast so that two hours later he was able to set off again with Jeremy and Richard.

James was soon left far behind, with the others heading for the open sea. And suddenly the reality of how big the waves really were dawned on them!

Eventually they bottled it and headed back to find James, who still hadn't managed to get more than a few yards from shore. Jeremy towed James away from the pier to the cheers of the crowd.

28

Then disaster looked set to strike, as the Dampervan floundered with no steering right in the path of a massive ferry. The Triumph's mast then broke again and was also in the path of the approaching ferry. Eventually the police arrived and ordered them all back to shore. Of course, this was easier said than done. Both the Triumph and the Dampervan had to be towed back to shore.

The Triumph was now damaged beyond repair.

It's dying, there's no doubt about it.

That's humiliating.

She's riding the waves like a twig.

I'm disappointed, I thought we were going to make it.

GLUG!

The Third Attempt

The wind had dropped and the sea was much calmer in time for the third attempt. The Dampervan was now powered by an outboard motor that Richard had bought from Jeremy for £1 million. And James was his cabin boy.

Jeremy was soon surging ahead.

Then the Dampervan began to take on water and within minutes, it had sunk.

This is the third time I've been in this ruddy sea.

It was Jeremy to the rescue again as he picked up both Richard and James on the way back to dry land. But this time Jeremy had a plan – they would attempt to break Richard Branson's record for crossing the Channel in a car, which stood at 1 hour 40 minutes 6 seconds.

Calais for lunch!

The lads were soon claiming that they were doing 125mph, and that brought a visit from the coastguard. The three intrepid sailors were asked to state their intentions. After declaring their plan to beat Branson's record, they were wished good luck.

Good luck and bon voyage!

Amazingly they kept ploughing on without mishap. Boldly going further than any pick-up had gone before, and bravely dodging the massive vessels in the shipping lanes.

I can't remember whose right of way it is!

Land ahoy!

What do we do now?

We're in **big trouble.**

It's **pouring in.**

Result

Then, having missed out on the record, but with just eight miles to go, they started to take on water. A lot of water. So James was sent to cling on to the front of the pick-up and act as ballast!

ARRRGGH!

Then, with the coast in sight, and the whiff of success playing in their nostrils, the waves started to get really big. Breakers were crashing over the Nissank and it looked like the sea would defeat them at the last moment.

I'm getting a bit **bored of sinking,** frankly.

We're **going down** boys.

We're **on the rocks.**

Come on, come on.

But then James bravely managed to tie a rope to the front bumper and with the help of some burly blokes on the shore, the Nissank was hauled in.

The pick-up had landed! Ok, so it had beached itself in Sangatte, not Calais, but it was still France!

Grow Your Own Petrol

Making petrol from crops – how hard can it be? Pretty much impossible if you don't know anything about the wonderful world of farming!

The team were sent away to do some research on the Internet, order some tractors and then get them delivered to the TG test centre. And what a collection of mechanical mammoths they ordered!

The ~~Cars~~ Tractors

First up was James with a £120,000 Fendt. It had a top speed of 31 mph and came with every toy imaginable. It included a computer that would keep it at a constant speed of 0.06 mph, which was perfect for Farmer Slow.

> It's the Mercedes S Class of agricultural vehicles.

> Jeremy's tractor was a JCB Fastrack something-or-other, which was packing a frightening 8.3 litre turbo-charged engine.

> That's a digger.

> No it isn't... this is the tractor that the army use.

> It didn't look that big on the computer to be honest.

> And then Richard's monster arrived. The Steiger had a top speed of 20 mph, caterpillar tracks and a 16 litre turbo-charged engine. Richard's tractor cost a massive £224,756 and weighed 24 tonnes.

It can't be **that** difficult.

The User-Friendly Test

The lads had to start their tractors, hitch them up to a trailer and reverse through the Top Gear car park. However, there were a number of expensive cars parked there, as well as some of the creations from previous shows.

James went first and was confronted with enough knobs and dials to fly a space ship! After an hour he still hadn't managed to get his tractor anywhere near the trailer so he gave up.

Jeremy was next and he soon had his engine running and trailer hitched. It was the reversing he couldn't quite get the hang of.

Richard is a bit of a country boy and bonded instantly with his hunk of agricultural hardware. Until he 'clipped' a very expensive Astra concept car.

How can you **crash** into your **own trailer?**

The **interesting** thing about Jeremy I find, is that he thinks problems can be solved by **shouting.**

I'm not a quitter, but I'm **quitting.**

Yeah, you see. I'm on a roll!

SSSKKRRREEEEEEE

Right, best to move on...

The Anti-Speed Test

The lads decided they'd all made a hash of the first task and that it was time to move on. The tractors were handed over to the Stig, who would then take them round the test track. But it was the **slowest** time, not the fastest, that would win.

James' rig lapped in at 3.28 seconds, while Richard's was even slower at 4.49 seconds.

In fact the laps were taking so long the lads all settled down for a spot of afternoon tea.

Jeremy got all excited that his JCB had gone round in just 2.57 seconds until he was reminded that the quicker your time the less points you got.

This is **excellent!**

It's all gone **quiet.**

Well, **how** do you commentate on a **tractor lap?**

Slow is **good** you fool!

Rubbish.

The Stig did have some trouble coping with Jeremy's tractor...

This is it, we're away in the most **ridiculous** drag race in history.

VRRRAAAAAAHHH

The Drag Race

The most important characteristics of a tractor are fuel efficiency, reliability and long service life. So to find out which tractor was best, the next challenge was a drag race. Although, not the kind of drag race you'd expect. The lads had to search round the Top Gear site and find some objects to tow. The heavier the object, the more points they earned. See? A *drag* race.

The convoy is snaking a **bit.**

Not **quite** as sprightly as I was hoping.

James hitched up a whole convoy of vehicles to his Fendt, including Jeremy's Toybota and Richard's original Dampervan. Richard decided to have a go at towing the TG production studio, even though it didn't have any wheels, while Jeremy went large and lined up at the start of the race towing a Boeing 747.

Despite losing the Renault Espace on the way James won, while poor Jeremy hardly left the start line.

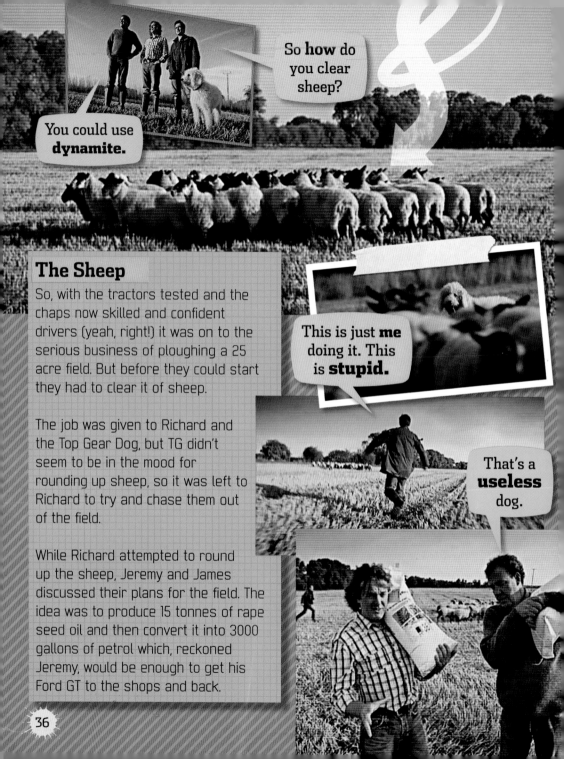

So **how do** you clear sheep?

You could use **dynamite.**

The Sheep

So, with the tractors tested and the chaps now skilled and confident drivers (yeah, right!) it was on to the serious business of ploughing a 25 acre field. But before they could start they had to clear it of sheep.

The job was given to Richard and the Top Gear Dog, but TG didn't seem to be in the mood for rounding up sheep, so it was left to Richard to try and chase them out of the field.

While Richard attempted to round up the sheep, Jeremy and James discussed their plans for the field. The idea was to produce 15 tonnes of rape seed oil and then convert it into 3000 gallons of petrol which, reckoned Jeremy, would be enough to get his Ford GT to the shops and back.

This is just **me** doing it. This is **stupid.**

That's a **useless** dog.

If he **falls in** I'm going to **die** laughing.

The Field

Eventually, using a proper dog to clear the sheep, the field was ready for ploughing. Until Jeremy discovered another problem - the only way into the field was over an old, rickety bridge. James managed to get over safely, but typically Jeremy broke it. After a very half-hearted attempt at mending it, Richard had to edge across with his tractor tracks hanging over the edge.

I can't see **anything**. I've **no idea** what it's doing.

Piece of **cake.**

And now for the ploughing. The field was divided into three equal sections and the team had no problems hitching up their tractors to the ploughs. Richard's kit looked like something taken from Battlestar Galactica – it was immense!

Have you **seen** the size of my **plough!**

VRMM VRUMM VRUM

37

This is going to be the fastest piece of ploughing **ever.**

I think this is the **first** thing we've **ever** filmed where **I** can do it and those two **can't!**

I'm **ploughing!**

The Ploughing

Then, having got their ploughs into position, they were off. Soon James was trundling along like Worzel Gummidge, while Jeremy was zigzagging across the field like a bat with no sense of direction.

It's **bad.**

Richard finally got the 'Starship Enterplough' to start but turning the mechanical beast around proved very tricky, and it soon ground to a halt. Meanwhile, rather than ploughing the field, it looked like James was digging it up.

CLANGG

Good, ploughing done.

Fire in the hole!

By now Jeremy was the only one still running but he soon got bored driving up and down, so he went for a classic Clarkson short cut – dynamite!

BA-DOOM

That's a **bit** tight.

Lunchtime. Richard was sent off, after much arguing about what exactly is in a ploughman's lunch, to buy food for the lads. However, driving his massive tractor through narrow village streets proved even more difficult than ploughing!

Before leaving town, Richard stopped to fill up – and it cost him a whopping £1,127!

I don't like the look of that **sky.** Not for **cultivating.**

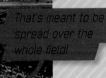

That's meant to be spread over the whole field!

The Result

Back at the field it was time to sow the seeds, which had to be distributed evenly over the whole field using a special machine. James insisted he was the man for the job. But he managed to dump it all in one spot and then just drove off! And then – just for once – it was Jeremy's turn to be livid.

Later, James was sent back to the field to distribute the seeds properly.

May, you're going to die! I'm going to **feed** you into your own **machine!**

A year later, they discovered that James had bought the wrong type of seeds and they now had 500 gallons of diesel instead of petrol. The only thing for it was to burn the diesel by entering a car in the Britcar 24 hour race. But that's a challenge for another time…

Build Your Own Car

> How hard can it **be** to build a **kit car?**

This challenge pitched the technical expertise of our Top Gear heroes against the driving skills of the Stig. So, a pretty unequal contest then!

The Challenge

The lads had to build a Caterham Seven Kit car in a garage at the Knockhill Racing Circuit in Scotland, while the Stig had to drive the same model up from Caterham HQ in Surrey, some 465 miles away. The first team to cross the start line would be declared the winner.

The trio were faced with a massive task and had very little technical knowledge to call on.

> **Of course** we are **ideally** suited to the job in hand.

> I trained as a local newspaper reporter, **Richard** trained as a local radio DJ, and **May** trained as a **pianist.**

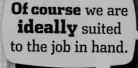

FN06 ACZ

Despite this, James soon took over the role of project leader. And as you'd expect, he insisted that everything was done by the book. The book being an instruction manual the size of the Oxford Dictionary. And that did Jeremy's head in!

We've only got **eight** hours, I can't read **that!** Rubbish – don't need that.

James, does it need a washer. **Yes or no?**

Shut up, Jeremy.

The lads were also using a satellite system to monitor the Stig's progress and soon discovered that he'd made an uncharacteristic mistake. Instead of taking the M25 he'd tried to go through the middle of London during rush hour, and had ended up in a huge traffic jam.

Jeremy was much happier once he'd found a hammer in the tool chest. He could then go around hitting things until they fitted!

Don't hit it with a hammer!

Why?

Because it's the tool of a **pikey**.

CLANGG

By now, Jeremy was losing heart. Basically, he likes driving cars, not building them. So he was told to start sorting out the car's interior and leave all the important mechanical bits to the other two.

Have I **got** to take it out?

Well, let's **think** about it!

Meanwhile on the M40, the Stig was starting to motor.

Then, brilliantly, Jeremy managed to fit one of the seats! It just happened to be facing the wrong way.

Glancing at the monitor, Jeremy noticed the Stig had stopped at services, and was revealing something new about himself. The Stig has a bladder.

He's at **Oxford** and we're putting the **engine** in. **Victory is ours!**

He's 299 miles away. At Stig speed that could be an **hour.**

Unfortunately, they were still trying to put the engine in over an hour later and the Stig was now well past Birmingham. The tension was starting to mount.

Can we **not** bicker now!

Even mild-mannered Richard was getting fed up and Jeremy was sacked from engine management.

Look at the picture.

It doesn't tell me **anything.**

It **does.**

Bored, bored, bored, bored...

The only thing that was really keeping the lads in it was that the Stig only had a small fuel tank and had to keep stopping for petrol.

Jeremy then had another go at the seats but this time he'd forgotten to attached the safety harness before doing up all the bolts.

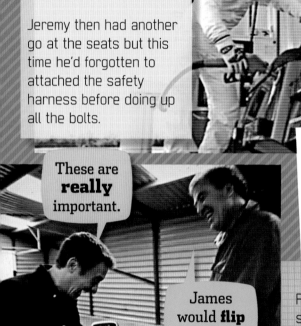

Every single thing I do is **rubbish.**

These are **really** important.

James would **flip** if he knew!

Fed up and bored, Jeremy began to take short cuts by not fitting all the washers and bolts. He let Richard in on his secret.

The Stig was now bearing down on them. But at least they'd got the electrics to work. And after more last minute fiddling, the car finally came to life, briefly....

Press the button.

It lives!

VRUMM

It's dead...

The Result

The Stig was now only a few miles away but to their utter amazement, the car had begun to turn over nicely. But there was no time to celebrate. The lads had a quick game of paper, scissors, stone to see who would drive the car. Jeremy won, clambered in and miraculously drove the Caterham over the start line.

Yes – that's enough. Victory! We've won.

But how? Where on earth was the Stig? Simple, he'd been caught speeding by the Scottish constabulary!

Does this car belong to you, sir?

Is the car stolen, sir?

It's a great experience.

I'd rather staple my ears to a horse.

As ever, the Stig reserved the right to remain silent, and was taken away to the police station for further questioning. Bet that was fun!

Back in the studio, the chaps had different opinions on this challenge.

Glossary

Asphalt

A thick, black goo that's mixed with sand or gravel to surface roads. A bit like Tarmac. It's rumoured that Jeremy is thinking of having his whole garden 'done in asphalt.'

Ballast

A heavy, dead weight that's used to give something more stability. See James' role aboard the Nissank in the Amphibious Car Challenge!

Boadicea

Warrior queen who chased the Romans out of England while sitting on a chariot that had huge spikes sticking out of the wheels. Some say her ghostly white spirit can still be seen charging around Lincolnshire today. Or is that the Stig?

Coupe

Type of car design that usually suggests something sporty and fast. Often with just two doors, and only enough leg room in the back for a small rodent, think of Jeremy's Fiat in the Police Car challenge.

Kit car

This is a car that comes in a kit form. This means that the driver has to buy a set of parts and put them together themselves. Something Jeremy will probably never do again. Ever.

Monte Carlo Rally

One of the most famous car races in the world, which was first run in 1911.

The Col De Turini is one of the most famous stretches of the course, and because the race is usually run in January, it's often covered in snow and ice. And if that wasn't enough, they drive it at night!

Ploughman's lunch

The ingredients of this cold British meal or snack can vary depending on who you ask. Basically it consists of a thick piece of cheese, relish, crusty bread and butter. Sometimes an egg, crisps or even beetroot might find there way onto the list as well.

Tunnel blasting

Take a big, powerful car into a long, deep tunnel. Next, put your foot down, sit back and enjoy the noise as all that power bounces back off the walls.

Turbo-charged

This means a car's engine has a nifty little gadget that forces more air into the cylinders to give it an extra bit of oomph.

Worzel Gummidge

Scruffy scarecrow that used come to life and star in a 1980s TV show. He was a bit slow and dim-witted, and rarely got anything right.

OLIZIA

IN JAIL NO ONE CAN HEAR YOU SCREAM